This Bible Is Presented To:

_____

On: _____

LHUMC DAYCARE
200 School Lane
Linthicum, MD 21090

The Story Bible

TYNDALE
FOR KIDS

Tyndale House Publishers Inc. • Wheaton, Illinois

Content selected and written by Meg Diehl. Illustrations copyright © 1996 by Lane Yerkes.
Design by Andrea Gjeldum.

Unless otherwise indicated all Scripture quotations are taken from the *Holy Bible*, New
Living Translation, © 1996. Used by permission of Tyndale House Publishers, Inc.,
Wheaton, Illinois 60189. All rights reserved.

Scriptures marked TEV are taken from the *Good News Bible* Old Testament, copyright ©
1976 by American Bible Society.

Scripture verses marked TLB are taken from *The Living Bible*, copyright © 1971 owned by
assignment by KNT Charitable Trust. All rights reserved.

Scripture verses marked SLB are taken from *The Simplified Living Bible*, copyright © 1990 by
KNT Charitable Trust. All rights reserved.

Scriptures marked NCV are taken from the *International Children's Bible, New Century Version*,
copyright © 1986, 1988 by Word Publishing, Dallas, Texas 75039. Used by permission.

Scripture quotations marked NIV are taken from the *Holy Bible*, New International
Version®. Copyright © 1973, 1978, 1984 by International Bible Society. Used by permission
of Zondervan Publishing House. All rights reserved. The "NIV" and "New International
Version" trademarks are registered in the United States Patent and Trademark Office by
International Bible Society. Use of either trademark requires permission of International
Bible Society.

LIBRARY OF CONGRESS CATALOGING-IN-PUBLICATION DATA

The Story Bible
   p. cm.
  Includes index.
  ISBN 0-8423-1323-0 (hc)
  1. Bible stories, English. [1. Bible stories.] I. Tyndale
House Publishers.
BS551.2.B4755 1995
220.9'505—dc20   94-43716

Printed in Mexico

01 00 99 98 97 96
 6   5   4   3   2   1

Contents

Note to Parents

THE MOST IMPORTANT STORY
your child will ever learn is the story found
in the Bible.

The Story Bible will introduce a child you love
to key biblical events, using actual words of
Scripture. By giving your child the big picture,
from Genesis to Revelation, *The Story Bible* provides the first step to a lifetime of Bible learn-
ing.

At the end of every story is a key idea. This
short statement helps your child understand
a specific truth of Scripture that is taught in
the story.

Complementing the Bible passage and the
key idea is the entertaining art of beloved
illustrator Lane Yerkes, which brings each
story to life.

Section introductions provide context for
the Bible stories, as well as simple transitions.

The Scripture Index at the back of *The Story
Bible* identifies the larger Bible passages from
which the selected verses have been taken.
Together, you and your child will be able to
look up these passages in a Bible as your
child's interest in each story grows.

May God richly bless your family as you
use *The Story Bible* to introduce the greatest
story ever written.

A LONG TIME A

no world. There was not even a sky

were no people either. Only God

that. Let's find out what happened.

GO THERE WAS

or a star in it. Of course, there

ived. God decided to change all of

God Makes the World

In the beginning God created the heavens
and the earth.

GENESIS 1:1, NIV

God made everything.

God Makes Adam and Eve

God created people in his own image; male
and female he created them.

from GENESIS 1:27, NLT

God made us and loves us.

Adam & Eve Live in the Garden of Eden

The Lord God planted a garden in Eden, in the East, and there he put the man he had formed. He told him, "You may eat the fruit of any tree in the garden, except the tree that gives knowledge of what is good and what is bad."

from GENESIS 2:8, 16-17, TEV

God provides for us and gives us rules.

Adam & Eve Disobey God

God asked, "Did you eat the fruit that I told you not to eat?" [Adam] answered, "I ate it." Then the Lord God said, "Man has knowledge of what is good and what is bad. He must not be allowed to take fruit from the tree that gives life, eat it, and live forever." So the Lord God sent [Adam and Eve] out of the Garden of Eden.

from GENESIS 3:11-12, 22-23, TEV

Adam and Eve broke God's rules. Now God must make things right again.

Noah Builds an Ark

The world was rotten to the core. God observed how bad it was. He said to Noah, "Go into the ark with your family. Bring the animals too . . . a pair each. One week from today I will begin forty days and nights of rain." Noah did everything the Lord commanded him.

from GENESIS 6:11-12; 7:1-5

God made a flood. Noah and his family and the animals were safe in the boat.

GOD CHOSE SOM

to teach you and me about his love and

were two of these people. They were

Israel. Many years later, an Egyptian

trouble for the people of Israel. He

read some of the verses from the Bible

how God helped the people of Israel.

SPECIAL PEOPLE

his commands. Abraham and Sarah

the first family in a nation called

king called Pharaoh began to make

made them slaves. Now you can

that tell about Abraham's family and

Abraham & Sarah Have a Baby

The Lord said, "Next year I will give you and Sarah a son!" Now Abraham and Sarah were both very old, and Sarah was long since past the time when she could have a baby. Then God did as he had promised, and Sarah became pregnant and gave Abraham a baby son. And Sarah declared, "All who hear about this shall rejoice with me. For who would have dreamed that I would ever have a baby?"

from GENESIS 18:10-11; 21:1-2, 6-7, TLB

We can trust God to keep his promises even when it seems like he can't.

Joseph Makes Up with His Brothers

Jacob loved Joseph more than any of his other children. But his brothers hated Joseph. They sold him, and traders took Joseph to Egypt.

Famine began, but in Egypt there was plenty of grain. Joseph was in charge of the grain. It was to him that his brothers came.

"Come here," Joseph said. "I am Joseph your brother! God turned into good what you meant for evil."

from GENESIS 37:3-4, 26-28; 41:54; 42:6; 45:4; 50:19-20, NLT

When people try to hurt us, God sees it and turns it into good.

God Cares about Israel

The Lord said, "I have seen the troubles my people have suffered in Egypt. I have come down to save them. I will bring them out of that land. I will lead them to a good land with lots of room, and I will be [their] God."

from EXODUS 3:7-8; 6:7, NCV

God sees our problems and helps us with them.

God Helps Moses Free Israel

Moses stretched out his hand over the sea, and the Lord drove the sea back with a strong east wind and turned it into dry land. The waters were divided, and the Israelites went through the sea on dry ground. And the Egyptians said, "Let's get away from the Israelites! The Lord is fighting for them."

from EXODUS 14:21-22, 25, NIV

God made a safe road for his people to walk on.

Moses Gets Ten Rules from God

The Lord said to Moses, "Come up to me
on the mountain. Stay there while I give
you the tablets of stone that I have [written]
with my instructions and commands. Then
you will teach the people from them."

EXODUS 24:12, NLT

God gives us rules to teach us.

GOD WANTED

Israel to have their very own country

Joshua and David, win battles with

the land God promised them. Ther

David and Solomon. You can read

THE PEOPLE OF

God helped some brave people, like

their enemies so that they could have

God gave Israel some kings, like

about some of their adventures.

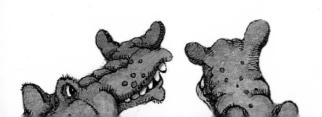

Joshua Fights the Battle of Jericho

At dawn of the seventh day they went around the city seven times. As the priests blew a long, loud trumpet blast, Joshua yelled to the people, "*Shout!* The Lord has given us the city!" Suddenly the walls of Jericho crumbled and fell before them, and the people of Israel poured into the city from every side and captured it! The Lord was with Joshua.

from JOSHUA 6:15-16, 20, 27, TLB

God is with us. He helps us do his work.

David Fights Goliath

The Philistines had a champion fighter named Goliath. Goliath shouted to the Israelite soldiers, "Choose a man and send him to fight me. If he kill[s] me, we will become your servants. But if I kill him, you will become our servants." [David] went to meet Goliath. Goliath saw that David was only a boy. He looked down at David with disgust. David said, "You come to me using a sword. But I come to you in the name of the Lord of heaven. You have spoken out against him. Today the Lord will give you to me." He put [a stone] into his sling and slung it. The stone hit the Philistine on his forehead, and Goliath fell facedown.

from 1 SAMUEL 17:4, 8-9, 40, 42, 45-46, 49, NCV

God is stronger than our enemies.

King Solomon Asks for Wisdom

"O Lord my God, you have made me king in place of my father David. But I am like a little child who doesn't know his way around. Please give me wisdom. Help me know what is right and what is wrong."

from 1 KINGS 3:7, 9, SLB

God helps us know what is right and what is wrong.

GOD CHOSE SO

(people who knew about God and

feelings toward us. God helped these

he wanted everyone to be able to

the words these wise people wrot

to be wise, too!

ME WISE PEOPLE

his ways) to write about God's

people know what to write because

earn about him. Reading some of

will help you

Do Not Do What Bad People Do

Oh, the joys of those who do not listen to
the advice of evil people! They do not hang
around with sinners. They do not laugh at
the things of God. They are like trees along
a river. They have sweet fruit each season.
Their leaves never get dry and fall off. All
that they do succeeds.

from PSALM 1:1, 3, SLB

*God wants us to obey his teachings. They will help us to
please him.*

God Forgives Us When We Do Bad Things

Happy is the person whose sins are forgiven. When I kept things to myself, I felt weak deep inside me. I moaned all day long. My strength was gone. Then I confessed my sins to you. I didn't hide my guilt. I said, "I will confess my sins to the Lord." And you forgave my guilt.

from PSALM 32:1, 3-5, NCV

God wants us to tell him when we do bad things. He wants to forgive us.

God Made Me

O Lord, you know everything about me. You made all the parts of my body. You put them together in my mother's womb. Thank you for making me so wonderfully! You saw me before I was born. You planned each day of my life before I began to breathe. How great to know you think about me all the time!

from PSALM 139:1, 13-14, 16-17, SLB

God knows all about me. He never stops thinking of me.

God Walks with Me

You clear the path ahead of me. You tell me where to stop and rest. Every moment you know where I am. You go in front of me. And you also follow me. You put your hand of blessing on my head.

from PSALM 139:3, 5, SLB

God is with me wherever I go.

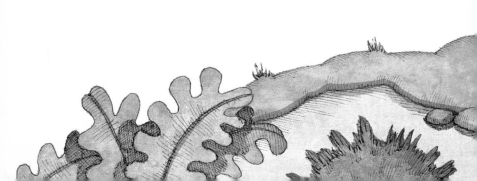

God Is a Good Shepherd

The Lord takes care of his people like a
shepherd. He gathers the people in his
arms. He carries them close to him. [The
Lord] gently leads.

from ISAIAH 40:11, NCV

God gently takes care of us.

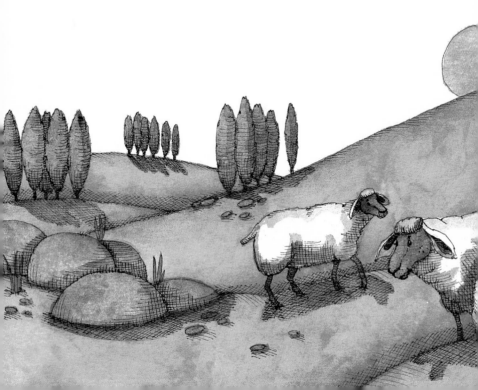

God Saves Daniel in the Lions' Den

The King issue[d] an edict: Anyone who prays to any god or man except to [the] King, shall be thrown into the lions' den.

When Daniel learned [this], he went to his window and prayed to God, just as he had done before. They brought Daniel and threw him into the lions' den. At dawn, the king hurried to the lions' den [and] called, "Daniel, has your God been able to rescue you from the lions?" Daniel answered, "My God sent his angel, and he shut the mouths of the lions." And when Daniel was lifted from the den, no wound was found on him, because he had trusted in his God.

from DANIEL 6:7, 10, 16, 19-23, NIV

God can be trusted to save us.

TO SHOW THE

world how much he loved them,

Jesus showed the world God's love

and what was wrong. Jesus cared

who were sick! Here's how it al

PEOPLE IN THE

God sent his very own Son, Jesus.

He taught people what was right

about people. He even healed people

started. . . .

An Angel visits Mary

God sent the angel Gabriel to Nazareth, a village in Galilee, to a virgin named Mary. The angel told her, "You will become pregnant and have a son, and you are to name him Jesus. The baby born to you will be holy and will be called the Son of God."

from LUKE 1:26-27, 30-31, 35, NLT

God promised that his Son, Jesus, would come to earth.

Mary Has a Baby

[Mary] gave birth to her first child, a son. She wrapped him in a blanket and laid him in a manger. This was because there was no room for them in the village inn. The child became a strong, robust lad. He was known for wisdom beyond his years. And God poured out his blessings on him.

from LUKE 2:7, 40, SLB

Jesus, God's perfect Son, was born into our world.

54

Jesus Is Baptized

One day, many people were being baptized.
And Jesus himself came and was baptized.
A voice from Heaven said, "You are my
much-loved Son. Yes, you are my delight."

from LUKE 3:21-22, SLB

God loves his Son, Jesus, and Jesus loves us.

Jesus Heals a Sick Man

Jesus met a man with an advanced case of leprosy. When [he] saw Jesus, he fell to the ground, begging to be healed. "Lord," he said, "if you want to, you can make me well again." Jesus reached out and touched the man. "I want to," he said. "Be healed!" And instantly the leprosy disappeared.

from LUKE 5:12-13, NLT

Jesus cares about our hurts and what makes us sad.

A Crowd Cheers for Jesus

The crowd in Jerusalem heard that Jesus
was coming. They took palm branches and
waved them. They shouted, "The Savior!
God bless the King of Israel!"

from JOHN 12:12-13, SLB

People said thank you to Jesus for all he had done.

MANY PEOPLE

But some people did not have love

and didn't believe he was God's Son.

were able to do it only because Jesus

to life! He proved that he was

taught was true.

LOVED JESUS.

in their hearts. They hated Jesus

They had Jesus killed, but they

let them. Then Jesus came back

God's Son and that everything he

Jesus Is Arrested

Judas came to the grove, guiding soldiers
and some officials from the chief priests
and Pharisees. They were carrying torches,
lanterns and weapons. Then the soldiers
arrested Jesus. They bound him and led
Jesus to the palace of the Roman governor.

from JOHN 18:3, 12, 28, NIV

Jesus was blamed for something he did not do.

Jesus Dies for Us

Pilate wanted to let Jesus go free. So he told
this to the crowd. But they shouted again,
"Kill him! Kill him on a cross!" Jesus and
two criminals were taken to a place called
the Skull. There the soldiers nailed Jesus to
his cross. Jesus said, "Father, forgive them.
They don't know what they are doing." At
three o'clock, Jesus died.

from LUKE 23:20-21, 33-34, 46, NCV

Jesus is perfect. He died to pay for all of our sin.

Jesus Lives

After the Sabbath there was a violent
earthquake, for an angel of the Lord came
down from heaven and, going to the tomb,
rolled back the stone and sat on it. The
angel said to the women, "Do not be afraid,
for I know that you are looking for Jesus,
who was crucified. He is not here; he has
risen, just as he said. Come and see the
place where he lay."

from MATTHEW 28:1-2, 5-6, NIV

Jesus is alive! He is stronger than death.

AFTER JESUS CA

he knew that he would soon be lea

He wanted to make sure everyone

So Jesus asked his special helpers, the

about the wonderful things he had

his friends began telling everybody

love spread far and wide.

ME BACK TO LIFE,

ving this world to live in heaven.

could still learn about God's love.

disciples, to tell people everywhere

done. When Jesus went to heaven,

about him! Soon the story of God's

70

Jesus Talks to His Friends

The disciples went to the mountain where Jesus had said they would find him. There they met and worshiped him. He told his disciples, "I have been given all power in Heaven and earth. So now go and make disciples in all the nations. Then teach these new disciples to obey all the commands I have given you."

from MATTHEW 28:16-20, SLB

Jesus visited his friends and told them to teach others about him.

Jesus Goes to Heaven

After he said this, [Jesus] was taken up before their very eyes, and a cloud hid him from their sight.

from ACTS 1:9, NIV

Jesus went back to God in heaven.

Jesus Is Coming Back

Look! He comes with the clouds of heaven.
And everyone will see him. He will remove
all of their sorrows, and there will be no
more death or crying or pain. Amen! Come,
Lord Jesus!

from REVELATION 1:7; 1:4; 22:20, NLT

*Jesus is coming back to earth. He will take us to live with
him forever, and he will take away all bad things.*

Scripture Index